Winter
WILDCRAFTS

Winter
WILDCRAFTS

INSPIRATIONAL PROJECTS HARVESTED FROM NATURE

TESSA EVELEGH

PHOTOGRAPHS BY DEBBIE PATTERSON

LORENZ BOOKS

First published in 1998 by Lorenz Books

LORENZ BOOKS are available for bulk purchase for sales
promotion and for premium use. For details write or call the
manager of special sales: Lorenz Books, 27 West 20th Street,
New York, NY 10011 Tel (800) 354-9657

Lorenz Books is an imprint of
Anness Publishing Inc.

ISBN 1 859657 756 8

Publisher: Joanna Lorenz
Editorial Manager: Helen Sudell
Designer: Nigel Partridge
Photographer: Debbie Patterson
Stylist: Tessa Evelegh

Printed and bound in Singapore

10 9 8 7 6 5 4 3 2 1

CONTENTS

INTRODUCTION

Beauty is Nature's coin, must not be hoarded,
But must be current, and the good thereof
Consists in mutual and partaken bliss...
Beauty is Nature's brag, and must be shown...

JOHN MILTON (1608-74)

Let nature's bounty be the inspiration for wildcrafts, and there will always be room for new ideas. Each month, new materials appear for free, and although they clothe the countryside at the same time each year, they still manage to

LEFT: Richly coloured apples are a clear sign that autumn has begun.

surprise, and the contrast with what has come before gives them fresh appeal. With the passing of twelve months, each fruit, flower, leaf or twig can be looked at in a completely new light, offering endless potential.

The sheer abundance of nature as she prepares for winter sets a creative challenge. You don't have to be a fine artist or sculptor to make something beautiful with the natural materials around at this time of year. Full ripe autumn fruits and vegetables in purples, greens, reds and oranges; golden ears of corn, shiny acorns and horse chestnuts; leaves glowing in vibrant fiery shades – what man-made material could provide such variety and so broad a palette?

The first step towards creating wonderful wildcrafts is to collect the material, and this in itself can be a great pleasure. Going for a walk is all the more enjoyable when you are on the lookout for beautiful shapes and colours, and all the more fulfilling when you return laden with bounty that you can transform into something fabulous for your home. While you are collecting, though, do bear in mind that one of nature's purposes at this time of year is to provide a store pantry for wildlife, so only collect

ABOVE: Fiery shades of reds and yellows, set off by the low sun, lend autumn a vibrant glow.

a tiny proportion of any fruit or nuts from the wild. You can always fill out arrangements with fallen leaves, orchard fruits, vegetables, corn, flowers and other cultivated produce. In deep midwinter, foliage such as fir, holly and ivy is marginally less vital to wildlife, but try to leave berries in the wild and use florist-bought berries to brighten the foliage.

As well as using fresh foliage, fruit and flowers, winter is the traditional time to use material preserved in late summer and early autumn. Everlasting flowers (flowers that can be dried), wind-dried grasses and seedheads, preserved leaves and dried fruits can be used to

great effect, and the long winter nights offer plenty of time for indoor creativity. Preserved materials add a new dimension to wildcrafts as they can be used to create more permanent items such as pictures, frames, and decorated accessories. Dried and pressed leaves can become printing blocks, as can cut fruits and vegetables such as apples, pears and potatoes.

The key to making beautiful things sourced from nature is to refrain from fussing. Keep the designs simple and let the beauty of the natural material speak for itself. Either use all of one kind of flower, fruit or foliage, or take inspiration from the hedgerows for colour combinations that will bring an ever-changing seasonal feel to your home.

The pages of this book are intended to inspire more than to instruct. This is a snapshot of the autumn and winter of one year, with over sixty wildcraft ideas put together during that time. Try them for yourself, or let them be a starting point for wildcrafts of your own, and fill your home with seasonal treats throughout the winter.

RIGHT: Fruits and flowers, berries and leaves all provide abundant pickings in autumn.

WILDCRAFT SKILLS

The joy of wildcrafting is its simplicity and any techniques needed are very quickly learned. At its simplest, you can just keep a jar of seasonal branches on the table to bring a little of the outside indoors. But wildcrafts also encompass careful observation and collection, preservation, carving and drying. The next few pages show you how to acquire all these skills and equip you with the know-how to make the projects in this book.

LEFT: Gathering together an interesting variety of natural materials is the enjoyable first step for all wildcrafts.

HARVESTING AND GLEANING

 Little surpasses the pleasure of a walk in the woods on a sunny autumn day. So searching for natural bounty in this, the richest hunting-ground of the season, must be one of autumn's greatest pleasures. As well as the deluge of fallen leaves, nature has plenty more delights in store: bright shiny horse chestnuts,

BELOW: Ornamental maize (corn) gives colourful structure to floral arrangements, wreaths and garlands right through the winter.

sweet chestnuts concealed in spiky hedgehog-like cases, neat acorns, cones and twigs. Collecting just a little of all the natural bounty at this time of year is a task children love to help with. Give them each a bag and they'll find delight in a woodland treasure hunt.

Less wild but no less bountiful for the wildcrafter is the autumn harvest. If you'd like to make sheaves and corn dollies, which are decorative figures made by plaiting (braiding) straw, now is the time to source long-stemmed wheat and barley. This is more difficult than you may think, as most grain crops have been bred with shorter stems in recent years. The very few farmers who grow long-stemmed varieties sell them directly to craft suppliers, who in turn quickly run out of stocks.

Autumn is also the time to look for ornamental maize (corn). The different varieties come in an astounding range of colours, from yellows, golds and reds through to russets, deep tans and black. Many of these are sold ready-dried. They look best when the papery leaves surrounding the grains have been left on so that you can peel them back to give the cobs the appearance of having diaphanous wings.

Orchard fruits are another material in plentiful supply for autumnal displays. Choose from purple plums dusted with a soft bloom, apples

ABOVE: A sheaf of barley is an enduring symbol of the harvest safely gathered in. Long-stemmed varieties of grain crops like this are usually available only from craft suppliers.

in greens, russet and reds or green or golden pears. All of them have wonderful rounded forms that add structure to any arrangement. Gather up windfalls – even a single garden tree can produce generous bowlfuls.

In hop-growing regions you may be able to

ABOVE: A seasonal treat in hop-growing regions, the pretty ballerina-like flowers of hops on the bine (vine) make a perfect garland.

LEFT: Apples and safe wild fungi make glorious wildcrafting materials.

buy fresh hop bines (vines) direct from the farm. With their delicate green flowers, these really are the most glorious plants. All the more precious because the season is short, bines make a fabulous decoration for seasonal celebrations.

As autumn turns to winter, look out for fir cones in all their varieties from tiny larch cones to larger pine cones. Berries of holly, pyracanthus and cotoneaster will also be putting on their best displays as winter progresses.

WORKING WITH FRUITS AND VEGETABLES

The sheer abundance of fruits and vegetables in autumn makes them an obvious material for seasonal displays and decorations. The variety is enormous, ranging from huge fiery red pumpkins to tiny shiny blackberries. All add colour and structure to displays.

BELOW: Draw a pattern on the skin before carving a pumpkin, then use a lino (linoleum) cutting tool with even pressure for clear, smooth lines.

There are many ways to use fruits and vegetables as decoration. Small fruits, such as blackberries and blueberries, can be put into pretty containers which can, in turn, become part of a larger display. Medium-sized fruits, such as apples, pears, plums and small gourds, can be wired with heavy-duty florist's wire and fastened into side displays, table centres, garlands and wreaths. It is best to choose under-ripe fruits as these have the double advantage of a longer "shelf life" and firm flesh that is easy to work with. Lend brightness and a mood of celebration by rubbing them with picture framer's gilt wax, putting on enough for a subtle shine yet allowing the natural tones of the fruit to show through.

Another way to use fruits decoratively is to carve them. Apples and pears, for example, are easy to carve: all you need is a small sharp kitchen knife to make simple geometric patterns. It is safer to choose slightly under-ripe pears as it is easier to cut clean lines on hard flesh than on soft. Immediately brush a little lemon juice over the cut areas to stop them from discolouring.

Large vegetables, such as pumpkins and squash, can stand alone as decorations, especially when carved and hollowed out to hold candles. The way you carve a pumpkin or squash

ABOVE: If you want to add a touch of brightness to an autumn display, rub fruits with picture framer's gilt wax. Wire the fruits with heavy-gauge florist's wire before securing them in arrangements.

depends largely on the variety you are using and the texture of its flesh. The contents of soft-fleshed types can be scooped out completely so that patterns cut out of the shell can be illuminated by a night-light (tea-light) placed inside. Some pumpkins have such hard flesh that it's almost impossible to remove. If yours are like this, you can use woodcarving or lino (linoleum) cutting tools to carve deeply into the skin, creating dramatic patterns that do not need to be lit up.

ABOVE: Vertical stripes always look smart on pears: use the finished fruits as part of a table decoration, or cook them for dessert.

RIGHT: Available in a wide variety of shapes and colours at this time of year, pumpkins and squash offer a huge variety of ornamental forms for carving. Their hues range from fiery orange tones to cool cream and blue-green; their shapes from a traditional cushion-like Cinderella pumpkin to flat pumpkins resembling deckle-edged patty pans.

PRESERVING LEAVES IN GLYCERINE

Leaves, the icons of autumn, continue to surprise year after year as they produce an astonishing array of colour. Their transformation from deepest green to orange, bronze, yellow and red, brings with it a wonderful depth and range of tones, as different parts of each leaf turn at different rates. Colours vie on a single leaf; still-green veins are picked out. Fortunately, there are several ways to capture the leaves' beauty while they're still at their best. The easiest is simply to collect them as soon as they fall from the trees and before they have had a chance to become soggy. Inside, they will dry naturally and curl a little, which gives them an extra dimension. You could also try preserving them in glycerine, pressing or skeletonizing them.

Foliage preserved in glycerine which is available from chemists (at drugstores), is left supple and fleshy rather than brittle and dry, though its colour is usually affected. Some varieties of leaves darken a little; others end up black, while most take on a coppery appearance. In some, the colour change becomes more apparent along the veins. Berries, buds and even acorns can be left on sprays of leaves and they, too, will be preserved along with the foliage.

It is important to use foliage while the sap is still rising, as it needs to be able to take up (absorb) the glycerine solution that will preserve it. As the water transpires out of the leaves, the glycerine replaces water in the veins, and preserves the foliage.

Add one part glycerine to two parts very hot water, shake it well and pour the mixture into a narrow-necked vase up to a depth of about 7.5cm/3in. To prepare the foliage, remove any damaged leaves, then cut the stems at an angle immediately before you put them in the container to ensure good take-up (absorption) of the solution. The leaves should be left in the solution for about 2-3 weeks, by which time they will be preserved and ready to use.

If the leaves become brittle rather than supple, this indicates that they were too old for this method because the sap was no longer rising so they were not able to take up the solution. Don't let this deter you from having another go, simply make sure your chosen leaves are quite supple and not too dried out and you will succeed.

LEFT: Pressed leaves add a decorative touch to family photographs.

ABOVE: To preserve foliage in glycerine, simply stand the prepared stems in a solution of glycerine for about 2 weeks. Gradually they will take up the glycerine, which will preserve them. If they have taken up most of the solution and you don't feel they are ready yet, simply add more to the container.

LEFT: When the leaves are ready, they will be supple with a slightly leathery feel, and are likely to have a coppery tinge. The veins will often be picked out in a darker colour.

15

PRESSING LEAVES

In autumn, glorious fiery oranges, golds and russet shades seem to invade the greens of summer, slowly displacing them in the process. So, in the mellow days of early autumn, the softened greens of late summer mingle with warmer tones all on the same leaf. The combinations can be irresistible and there's always a temptation to capture and preserve them.

LEFT: Autumn leaves retain their vibrant colours even when pressed.

Happily, leaves are just about the most suitable candidates for pressing, which is one of the easiest ways to preserve plant material. Being flat and, by autumn, a little dried out anyway, the job is partly done from the outset. Thankfully, too, they usually retain their vibrant colours during the process. Choose leaves with pretty shapes, such as sycamore, oak or maple, selecting those that are undamaged and showing the most striking colours. They should not be too dry as they will be brittle and could be damaged while being pressed, so newly fallen leaves are the best and it is a great children's game to try to catch them as they fall from the tree.

If you don't have a purpose-made flower press, place them between sheets of blotting paper and then put heavy books on top of them. A neat way to press a quantity of leaves is to place a layer of leaves between each page of an artist's watercolour book. Put some heavy books on top to keep the layers flat. Leave the weights on the leaves for several days before checking them. The leaves are ready when they are perfectly flat and completely dried out so they can retain their shape when held upright. If they are not ready, put them back under the weights for

ABOVE: The warm tones of crab apples add form and texture to autumn table displays.

a few more days. Pressed leaves are very brittle, so they'll need to be handled with care when you are working with them. They should be stored flat in a box between sheets of tissue paper until you are ready to use them. The leaves can be used to decorate the pages of photograph albums, or mounted on textured handmade papers.

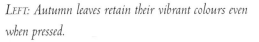

SKELETONIZING LEAVES

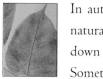

In autumn, leaves often become naturally skeletonized as they rot down on the damp forest floor. Sometimes, all the fleshy parts of some of the leaves erode away, leaving only a delicate leaf-shaped skeleton of veins. The beauty of these has long been recognized,

BELOW: To speed up the skeletonizing process, boil the leaves in a detergent solution.

though it is rare that the whole outline of a leaf is preserved intact by this natural process. Over the years, ways have been sought to mimic the look while retaining the shape. The traditional way to make skeletonized leaves is to put the leaves in a container of rainwater for several weeks until the softer tissue begins to rot. The flesh can then be brushed away using a small brush such as a toothbrush.

Nowadays, it is easy to speed up the process. Put a cup of washing detergent into a pan of water and add the leaves. Bring the pan to the boil, then simmer for about half an hour. Take the leaves out, rinse them in cold water, then carefully brush away the tissue with a soft toothbrush to leave the filigree leaf shapes. If the end result is a little dingy, you can brighten them up by soaking the finished leaves in a weak solution of bleach, and then rinsing them thoroughly.

Skeletonized leaves look very delicate, and indeed, they don't stand rough treatment. However, they are remarkably attractive, and can be used in many ways. Rub them with picture framer's gilt wax and frame them for simple but striking wall decorations. Put them under fine tulle on a dining table to make a pretty table covering, or use them as a natural doily under petits four, fondants or chocolates on a glass

ABOVE: Skeletonized leaves look wonderful whether left natural or rubbed with a little picture framer's gilt wax, as here.

plate. Add skeletonized leaves to flower arrangements, or even use them for decoupage, gluing them to the surface of a box or piece of furniture, then varnishing over them, thin layer after thin layer, until they almost seem to be part of the original object.

WORKING WITH WINTER CITRUS

Some of the best citrus varieties do not ripen until well into the winter, so these bright, sweet-smelling fruits have long been established as one of the treats of the season. As well as being of culinary value, oranges and lemons have been used for decorative purposes since medieval

BELOW: It's easy to create intricate patterns on lemons using a cannelle knife (fine linoleum cutting tool).

times, and even now they lend a seasonal air to any arrangement. Used fresh in wreaths, garlands and table displays, they have a crisp, modern look; dried, they acquire a more traditional feel.

One of the best known and loved decorative uses for oranges is to make them into pomanders that will last the winter through. The traditional method of making these is to stud the oranges with cloves, roll them in orrisroot powder, then dry them over a period of several weeks. This takes time and can be a bit haphazard, as in the process the pomanders can become mildewed. A much quicker and more reliable method is to dry them out in an oven (preferably a fan-assisted one). When the pomanders come out, their skins retain a leathery suppleness and are not quite as hard and dark as with traditional slow drying. This method works just as well with other tight-skinned citrus, such as lemons, kumquats and the paler-skinned limes.

To dry citrus fruits, slit the skins to allow the hot air to reach the flesh and dry it out more quickly. The prepared fruits then need to be stuck kebab-style on to skewers. Rest the ends of the skewers on the edges of a deep roasting pan so the oranges are suspended and the air can circulate all around them. Place the whole ensemble in an oven pre-heated to

ABOVE: The skin of the fruit needs to be slit so that the warm air in the oven can reach into the flesh to dry it.

BELOW: Push a skewer through the orange at a point where the skin is slit so as not to spoil the design.

ABOVE: Use cloves to decorate pomanders with traditional geometric designs or simple motifs.

110°C/225°F/Gas ¼ and leave for up to 12 hours, or until the fruits are dried out.

A rather quicker and simpler way to decorate citrus fruits is to carve them. You'll need a cannelle knife (fine linoleum cutting tool), which is designed to cut fine grooves in fruits and vegetables. Choose firm fruits such as lemons that provide a good resistance against the knife, as this results in clean cuts. It is easiest to start by cutting a single spiral around the fruit or vertical lines to make stripes, before progressing to intricate designs. If you have a zester with a row of tiny holes, you could use this instead to make evenly spaced fine lines, perhaps progressing to chequer-board designs. As well as using the finished lemons for purely decorative purposes, you could cut them into quarters to use as an unusual garnish for fish dishes or desserts.

MAKING WINTER DECORATIONS LAST

Encouraging fresh decorations to last as long as possible is a priority at any time of the year. It's especially important in winter if you want the display to last through any festivities. Fortunately, a lot of evergreen material has thick stems which hold a substantial amount of water, and this, combined with the low level of evaporation in cold weather, means you're off to a good start. Cut branches of foliage such as holly and pine can last up to a couple of weeks outside, even out of water.

Most important for a lasting display is a good foundation. Start by soaking florist's foam thoroughly, then let it drain before cutting it up

ABOVE: Single blooms can be placed in orchid phials (vials) which can then be wired into stair swags or garlands where it is impossible to use florist's foam.

to create the base. Larger pieces will hold the water for longer, and in the case of a mantel garland, for example, you can simply cut the foam into two lengthways. Once it is cut, lay it out to make sure you are satisfied with the shape it makes, then wrap it up in a strip of chicken wire.

If you are making a door wreath, you may want smaller pieces of foam to make a smoother circle, or you may prefer to buy a ready-made wreath base from the florist. Arrange the foliage and flowers in the base, then spritz it generously using a garden or ironing spray. Once you have hung the wreath, spritz it regularly (at least every

day) to moisten the foliage and keep it from drying out. That way it should last a fortnight.

If you want to use flowers in places where you cannot use a florist's foam base (such as on a stair garland) buy some orchid phials (vials) from the florist and place a bloom in each one.

BELOW: Thick-stemmed evergreens, such as this variegated holly, will stay fresh-looking even out of water during the cold damp weather of winter.

BELOW: Make up a base of well-soaked florist's foam wrapped in chicken wire. Make it up in its final position to make sure you get the dimensions right.

ABOVE: To prolong the life of the display, remember to spritz it with water every day.

LEFT: A little attention every day will keep indoor displays fresh for up to 2 weeks.

FRUITFUL
EARLY
AUTUMN

Season of mists and mellow fruitfulness,
Close bosom-friend of the maturing sun;
Conspiring with him how to load and bless
With fruit the vines that round the thatch-eaves run.

JOHN KEATS (1795-1821)

ABOVE: Autumnal fruits and flowers in perfect harmony.

LEFT: In early autumn, the orchard fruits are ready to harvest.

Autumn is the season of abundance. Leaves still adorn the trees and shrubs, but now they share the laden boughs with plump, ripe fruits, berries and seedcases. The hedgerows are bright with full red rosehips and glistening juicy blackberries, and entwined with the soft fluff of old-man's-beard (*Clematis vitalba*). As summer turns to autumn, the earth is still warm and some garden plants, such as Michaelmas daisies (*Aster*), chrysanthemums and Japanese anemones (*Anemone hupehensis*) have yet to bloom.

While there's a sense of pathos when we feel the first nip in the morning air that marks the end of summer, nature herself seems to rejoice

BELOW: Glistening rosehips are nature's own jewels, adorning the hedgerows.

as misty mornings and autumn rainfall give her a last chance to swell the fruit and produce the intense colours of autumn foliage and flowers. Early autumn offers a glorious palette of deep purples, burgundies, russet, oranges and greens. As flowers such as hydrangeas, left over from the summer, gently dry on their stems, their bright pastel pinks and blues mellow to softer shades of old rose and russet.

The other enduring image of early autumn is the harvest. Sheaves of golden corn and the sweet smell of fully ripened apples, pears and plums symbolize the fruition of the year's work. Since humans first began to cultivate the land, harvest has been the time when farming communities could take stock and assess whether there was plenty of food to take them through the winter, or whether the times ahead would be hard. In farming communities of times gone by, when a good harvest was believed to lie in the lap of the gods, many rituals and traditions grew up around the harvest.

It was thought that the corn spirit retreated as the field was harvested, and came to rest in the last sheaf where it would sleep through the winter. The corn spirit needed to be pleased, so this last sheaf would be cut and plaited (braided) into a corn dolly (decorative straw figure), then given a place of honour in the local

ABOVE: Ornamental cabbages are at their best in autumn, in gorgeous shades of blue-green and purple.

tavern. The following spring, the sheaf would be brought back to the field at seed time so the spirit could again bring about the germination of the new crop.

Once the crops had been gathered in, there was great jubilation as the Harvest Home was celebrated, with the farmer treating the workers to much eating, drinking and merriment. Farming and country communities still celebrate

ABOVE: Collect apples before strong autumn winds blow them off the trees.

RIGHT: Newly picked plums have an evocative dusty-looking bloom.

their year's achievement with village fairs, staging competitions for the largest or most perfect specimens of all manner of fruit and vegetables. Harvest Festival is also an important date in the church calendar when thanks are given to God in village churches for the bounteous gifts that fill granaries and larders.

This is the time for seasonal displays of sheaves and corn dollies (decorative straw figures), and fresh arrangements that combine the full richness of autumn: glorious fruit and vegetables amongst the season's leaves and flowers.

TRADITIONAL CORN DOLLY

Despite their intricate appearance, corn dollies (decorative straw figures) are not difficult to make once you have mastered the art of working a five-straw plait (braid). Corn dollies can be made from many types of straw, but the best is long, hollow-stemmed wheatstraw. Look for ones with the longest section from the ear to the first "knot" where the leaf parts from the stem.

MATERIALS

sheaf of long hollow-stemmed wheat
secateurs (pruners) or scissors
short length of raffia
2 dried oak leaves

1 To prepare the straws: remove the leaves, cut off each straw just above the first knot, then soak them in water for about 15 minutes. Remove the straws from the water, then stand them upright to drain. Tie five straws together near the ears using raffia. With the ears pointing downwards, spread out the straws like the spokes of a wheel. Working anti-clockwise (counter-clockwise), pass the first straw over the next two straws (the second and third), to occupy the space between the third and fourth straws. Go back one straw (to what is the third straw) and pass this straw over the next two straws.

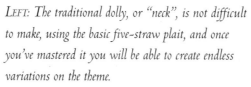

LEFT: The traditional dolly, or "neck", is not difficult to make, using the basic five-straw plait, and once you've mastered it you will be able to create endless variations on the theme.

2 Then go back one straw and pass that straw over the next two straws. If you were to continue in this way, you would end up with a basic five-straw plait (braid), but to create the shape of this dolly, you need to begin to widen it out.

3 To widen out the shape, carefully bend the first straw over the second to lie outside the third straw. This is to ensure the fold in the first straw is facing away from the plait to begin to widen it.

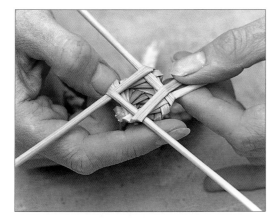

4 *Then bring the first straw just inside the third, butting the first straw up to the edge of the bend in the third straw. Continue making rounds in this way, and you will find the dolly gradually widens out.*

5 *When you get to the end of a straw, snip it near a corner. Insert a new straw inside the hollow of the old one and continue to plait (braid). When you want to narrow the dolly, bring each successive corner fold to the inside of the last, just as it was brought outside the last to widen. Once it has narrowed down to a point, finish with a long straight plait, loop it around and tie. Trim with oak leaves.*

WHEATSHEAF TRADITIONS

The simplest wheatsheaves are the most beautiful. Long straight straws tied in the middle with twine make a balanced and pleasing sheaf. This simple image has come to symbolize the harvest, which probably adds to its universal appeal. However, it is also traditional to add other autumn foliage, nuts and flowers for more elaborate sheaves whose beauty lies in their varied textures.

RIGHT: A sheaf of oats, oak leaves and maize, tied to a gatepost or fence, makes a pretty and lasting seasonal welcome for autumn visitors.

BELOW: To make the sheaf, first tie the oak branches on to the oats using raffia, then add the maize (corn). Add the decorative seagrass binding only once you're sure the sheaf is secure.

ABOVE: Barley, with its feathery ears and long straight stems, makes a striking sheaf. Twist the stems slightly to make them splay out at the top and bottom — both for greater impact and to give the whole ensemble a stable foundation. This sheaf has been tied with raffia, then given a belt of a five-strand plait (braid) made of seagrass as a final elegant detail.

LEFT: To make the seagrass plait, tie five strands together at one end, then lay them all parallel to each other over your hand. Take the right-hand strand and weave it over and under the other strands. Take the strand that is now furthest to the right and repeat, and so on, keeping the plait as taut as you can. Finish by tying the ends together in a knot.

HOP MANTEL GARLAND

 Hop bines (vines) are gloriously wild-looking, with delicate green flowers that seem to dance along their full length. Reaching up to 7m/23ft, bines make an ideal base for an autumn garland, whether it's around a door or across a mantel for a party, or over a church porch or churchyard gate for a wedding. Look out for them in early autumn when they are being harvested, as they are more pliable while they are still fresh. Hops are also available dried and can be revived and made more pliable with a spritz of water just before you are ready to arrange them.

MATERIALS
hooks or nails
hammer
pliers
florist's reel wire
hop bine (vine)
12 or more hard Conference pears
picture framer's gilt wax
heavy-gauge stub (floral) wires

RIGHT: Golden pears, with their curvaceous lines and smooth skins, make an excellent foil for the delicate-looking pale green hops.

1 Arrange hooks, nails or other suitable attachments either side of the fireplace. Use florist's reel wire to secure the complete bine (vine) to the mantel shelf.

2 Using your fingers, rub each pear all over with picture framer's gilt wax, allowing a little of the pear's natural skin tones to show through.

3 Pass a heavy-gauge stub (floral) wire through the base of each pear and twist the ends together. Use the wires to attach the pears to the bine base by winding them around the stems of the bine.

CABBAGE CANDLE RING

 In autumn, there's a wide choice of ornamental cabbages, with leaves in wonderful colour combinations. Here, blue-green leaves shot with purple have been used to make a simple but striking candle-ring.

MATERIALS
kitchen knife
florist's foam block
pillar candle
plate
ornamental cabbage

1 Cut a square block from the florist's foam large enough to fix the candle in, leaving a margin of about 1cm/½in all round. Thoroughly soak the foam in water, allow to drain and place it in the middle of the plate, then push the candle into the centre.

LEFT: *Purple veins make a stunning tracery pattern in blue-green cabbage leaves.*

2 Trim away the top edge of the block all around the candle. Break the leaves off the cabbage and, working from the bottom, push them face up into the sides of the florist's foam.

3 For the top layer, have the underside of the leaves uppermost to make them fan away from the candle.

AUTUMN SIDE DISPLAY

The soft greens and purples of early autumn make for breathtaking displays, and at this time of year there's a wonderful variety of flowers and fruits as well as foliage to work with. This arrangement combines all three, using tiny terracotta pots to add structure as well as to contain the smaller fruits.

MATERIALS
2 blocks florist's foam
kitchen knife
large bowl
4 small terracotta pots
secateurs (pruners)
bunch of oak leaves
blackberries and blueberries
3 ornamental cabbages
3 artichokes
3 flowering artichokes

RIGHT: Cabbages, blueberries and artichokes, usually more at home on the greengrocer's stall, make a voluptuous autumn display.

1 Soak the florist's foam and cut it to fit the bowl. Arrange the pots in the bowl, pushing them into the foam. Add stems of the oak leaves all around the edge of the bowl.

2 Fill the terracotta pots with the blackberries and blueberries. Position the ornamental cabbages in between the pots of fruit.

3 Complete the arrangement with the artichokes.

HYDRANGEA FRUIT BOWL

The colours of hydrangea flowers gradually soften as summer turns to autumn, fading into increasingly subtle tones. The green varieties retain a verdant quality, even when they are fully dried, while the more colourful summer blooms take on fabulous old rose shades. These are colours that look glorious with autumn fruit such as plums and figs, so here they have been used to create an unusual presentation for an attractive autumn dessert.

MATERIALS
florist's foam ring, 40cm/16in in diameter
green serving plate
10 hydrangea heads and leaves
secateurs (pruners)

1 Soak the florist's foam ring in water. Place the plate in the middle of the ring. Cut the hydrangea stems to about 2.5cm/1in.

2 Arrange the hydrangea heads in the ring to cover the foam and add a few leaves for relief.

LEFT: *Purple and green may seem an unlikely colour combination, but here it is arresting.*

ROSEHIP WREATH

By early autumn, rosehips have ripened to their glorious best. Climbing and rambling roses produce long trailing branches of pretty rosehips that can easily be twisted into an enchanting wild-looking wreath. Be careful of any sharp thorns when you are working.

MATERIALS
florist's reel wire
trailing stems of rosehips
secateurs (pruners)

1 Using the wire, bind together the ends of two long stems of rosehips.

2 Bind the other two ends together to make a circle. You may wish to use three stems to make up the circle.

3 Add extra stems where the wreath needs extra fullness by twisting them into the frame.

LEFT: Varieties of roses that have attractive glossy rosehips like these should not be dead-headed in the summer if you want the hips to develop.

DECORATIVE FRUIT

 Fruit is abundant in autumn, and symbolic of the season, so use it in witty and decorative ways — both for table and side displays and for imaginative food decorations. The seasonal glut makes this inexpensive and even if you make a mistake the fruit won't be wasted: you can just eat it, juice it or use it in cooking delicious fruit pies and tarts.

RIGHT: Carved lemons look pretty displayed in a bowl and can make a decorative garnish. Carve them using a cannelle knife (fine linoleum cutting tool). Make swirly patterns like these, or try geometric checks, which look just as effective.

BELOW: Serve pears a cut above the rest by carving stripes on them with a sharp paring knife. Brush lemon juice on to the cut areas to keep the flesh white.

RIGHT: Symbolic of love, apples make a witty display when given lips. Choose apples that do not have too high a sheen, but do have an attractive colour combination such as russet and green so the lips show up well. Apply a generous layer of russet-orange lipstick to your own lips and kiss the apples to make an imprint. Tuck each one in a basket and arrange them in a group.

FRUIT PRINT CALICO CUSHION

Very effective yet incredibly easy to do, fruit shapes in autumn shades look crisp and modern when printed on simple calico cotton. This cushion has a different design on each side, using the same apple and pear motifs for a co-ordinated look.

MATERIALS

2 x 50cm/20in squares of calico, plus a spare piece

fabric paint in apple green, yellow and bronze

apple cut in half lengthways through stem and core

pear cut in half lengthways through stem and core

damp cloth

fabric pen in dark brown or black

sewing machine

matching thread

scissors

iron

30cm/12in square cushion pad

tailor's chalk

RIGHT: A more random design lends a fifties' feel.

1 Try out the printing on spare calico. Then smear the apple green or yellow fabric paint on to the cut surface of the fruit and print on to the cloth. Allow to dry.

2 Wipe the fruit clean using a damp cloth, apply the bronze paint and make a trial print on the cloth on top of the first print. Allow to dry.

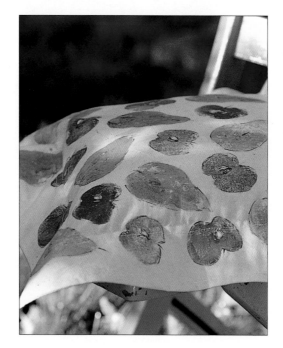

3 Using the pen, sketch around the edge of each fruit print and also mark out the pip (seed) area. Use the pen lightly, allowing it to skip in places so the line is not too dark and hard.

4 *Plan and print the design on the calico squares. Allow to dry. With right sides together, sew around three sides. Trim the corners, iron the seams open and turn through to the right side. Slip the cushion pad in and centre and mark the position of the edges of the cushion with tailor's chalk, making sure the pad is centrally placed.*

Take the cushion pad out and top-stitch through all layers around the same three sides as before. Replace the pad. Turn in and slip-stitch the raw edges of the open end to close. Top-stitch all around just inside the outside edge. Top-stitch the fourth inner seam and top-stitch a second line of stitching all around just outside the inner line.

RIGHT: Simple lines of apples and pears make for a crisp modern design.

ROSEHIP TREE

Gather a variety of rosehips from around the garden, then turn them into a delightful little tree to decorate house, garden or patio. You'll need a stout pair of gardener's gloves, as many of the best hip-bearing shrub roses also have vicious thorns. Make this using wet florist's foam and it should last about a week.

MATERIALS
kitchen knife
florist's dry foam block
terracotta pot
bundle of willow osiers (branches)
secateurs (pruners)
florist's foam block or ball
gardener's gloves
selection of rosehips
moss

1 Cut the dry foam to fit securely in the pot. Trim the willow osiers (branches) to about 45cm/18in. Grasp them together at the bottom and push them into the centre of the foam in the pot.

LEFT: Rosehips from varieties such as 'Hansa', which are full and red, make a wonderful material for any autumn arrangement.

2 Soak the other piece of florist's foam. If you are using a ball, simply push this on to the tops of the sticks. If you are using a block, first trim it to a ball shape before soaking.

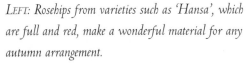

TIP
This beautiful rosehip tree will brighten any hallway or make a welcome decoration on your doorstep.

3 Wearing gloves, trim the branches of rosehips and push them into the foam. Cover the ball completely.

4 Dress the top of the pot with moss.

JARS OF AUTUMN COLOUR

 Autumn, like the sunset, puts on a glorious bright show, as if in an attempt to make up for the darker times that are to come. Yellows, golds, russet and the last of the greens vie for attention with the reds and oranges of berries and fruits. Autumn displays look best when they are not too mannered: just put them into jars and let them be.

BELOW: Branches of crab apples combine fabulously with russet beech leaves.

LEFT: A jug of Chinese lanterns (Physalis), with their enchanting orange fruits set against green leaves, always makes an eye-catching autumn arrangement.

ABOVE: Autumn berries will happily mix. Here, a jar of waxy, translucent berries of the guelder rose (Viburnum opulus) is set off by a jar of mountain ash (rowan).

LEFT: Hydrangeas fade into subtle sepia tones during autumn. Here, several varieties have been combined with seasonal red berries for a pretty early autumn display.

CRAB APPLE TABLE DECORATION

Crab apples have a special charm and the cultivated varieties produce fruit in a range of glorious colours. They make wonderful material for wild-looking arrangements such as this candle-ring. Make it up in wet florist's foam, and then let the whole thing dry out for a lasting autumn arrangement.

MATERIALS

florist's foam ring, 25cm/10in in diameter

4 yellow ochre tapered candles

secateurs (pruners)

2 branches crab apples

3 branches pin oak (*Quercus palustris*) leaves

1 Soak the florist's foam ring. Set the candles, evenly spaced, into the foam. Using sharp secateurs (pruners), cut the small branches of crab apples off the main stems. Arrange the oak leaves around the ring.

2 When the ring is covered with oak leaves, add smaller sprays to the inside.

3 Add the bunches of crab apples.

LEFT: The yellows and russet of the crab apples and pin oak leaves are emphasized by the yellow ochre of the four tall, slim candles.

LATE
AUTUMN
GOLD

Fair is the world, now autumn's wearing,

And the slippard sun lies long abed;

Sweet are the days, now winter's nearing

And all winds feign that the wind is dead.

WILLIAM MORRIS (1834-96)

ABOVE: A simple satin bow adds the finishing touch.

*LEFT: The woods are at their most beautiful in the mellow midday autumn sun —
the perfect time to collect natural craft materials.*

Falling leaves are the enduring symbols of late autumn. They take on the most astounding colours, with vibrant oranges and golds marrying themselves to the greens of summer, and lighting up the horizon with their fiery colours.

Although the weather will really have broken by now, clear autumn days have a beauty all of their own. The low sun shines with a golden light, casting softer and longer shadows than in the brighter, harsher light of summer.

There is plenty to be harvested and preserved right now. The combination of the drying effect

LEFT: Golden autumn leaves are a universal icon of autumn.

BELOW: The gradual change into their autumn colours and dappled golden light combine to show the leaves at their most beautiful.

ABOVE: Oak leaves and acorns are to be found in plentiful supply in forests in the late autumn months.

of late summer and the slowing of growth in autumn means that much material is already semi-preserved. Capture the colours by pressing leaves for mounting in picture frames or between the pages of photograph albums, or even use them as natural decoupage. If you'd prefer more dimension for floral arrangements or temporary decorations for celebrations, let them air-dry into their own natural gently curled forms.

As shrubs and trees are stripped of their leaves, sticks and twigs become prominent again, just as they were in the spring — notably the rich burgundy red of the straight whip-like branches of dogwood (*Cornus*). Collect a few to make bird tables and houses, tea trays or decorative boxes.

Late autumn is also the season for pumpkins, squash and gourds, which come in a glorious array of colours from hot red to cool blue-greens. These can be simply piled up for autumn displays, or carved for seasonal celebrations.

As the nights draw in, late autumn is the ideal time to put preserved summer material to good use by making wreaths, topiaries and arrangements from dried flowers and grasses.

QUICK LEAFY DECORATIONS

The glorious shades and sheer abundance of leaves in autumn make them an irresistible material for use in decorations. The advantage they have over summer leaves is that, being dried out by the time they fall, they will retain their beauty for considerably longer. Use leaves for table or window decoration when entertaining, or for special autumn celebrations. Although autumn leaves are surprisingly resilient and will last some time if handled with care (or preferably not handled at all), they will eventually crumble, so enjoy them while they last.

ABOVE: Decorate an autumn table with a cloth made from finest golden tulle laid over a scattering of autumn leaves.

LEFT: Give glasses a party feel by tying large oak leaves around them with pieces of the finest green raffia or similar twine. This looks especially good on amber-coloured tumblers.

RIGHT: Create a natural curtain by tying bundles of autumn leaves together and hanging them at the window on fine twine. More leaves can be stuck lightly to the window frame to give the impression they are falling to the ground. Attach the leaves with sticky tack, using the smallest blob at either end of the main stem or vein.

WOODLAND TOPIARY

There's something immensely appealing about oak leaves and acorns, probably linked to fairy tales we heard as children. There are plenty of acorns to be gathered in the autumn, both in the countryside and in city parks. You'll need to collect small sprays of leaves, some complete with their acorns.

MATERIALS
florist's dry foam ball, 10cm/4in in diameter
10cm/4in terracotta pot
oak leaf sprays
pliers
acorns
heavy-gauge stub (floral) wires

1 Place the foam ball in the pot. Prepare the leaves by trimming the stems to 1cm/½in. Try to retain acorns on as many sprays as possible.

3 Cut each stub (floral) wire into three equal lengths and push one into the base of each loose acorn and bend the end downward.

2 Make a ring of leaves around the top of the pot.

LEFT: *These acorn cups make an interesting alternative to the common smoother ones.*

4 Push the wired acorns into the florist's foam. Continue adding leaves and acorns until the foam ball is completely covered.

WILLOW BIRD TABLE

This enchanting wigwam-style bird table made from willow twigs is ideal for smaller birds. It's easy to make, and the raffia used to bind it should hold through the winter, though you may like to re-bind the table for next winter before the raffia begins to disintegrate.

MATERIALS

secateurs (pruners)

large bundle of willow osiers (branches)

raffia

1 Cut 32 lengths of willow 23cm/9in long from the osiers (branches). Fold a length of raffia in half and place the end of the first stick in the fold. Twist the two ends of the raffia and place another stick next to the first. Continue weaving in this way until you have used 24 sticks. Tie the raffia ends. Weave more raffia around the other ends of the sticks to create the base.

2 Place another stick on top of the base, along the woven line. Take another piece of raffia, fold it in half and place the fold over the loose stick, passing the two ends between the base sticks and either side of the original weaving.

3 Turn the whole thing over and tie together as shown. Now pass one end between the next two sticks, over the loose stick and back to the underside of the base. Tie. Continue until the whole length of the reinforcing stick has been bound firmly to the base. Repeat at the other end. Next, make the short table walls. Place a stick across the ends of the bound-on sticks and tie at the corners using raffia. Repeat at the other end. Repeat with another pair of sticks placed at right-angles to the first, in line with the bound-on sticks. Finally, tie on another pair at right-angles again.

LEFT: Made only with natural materials, this bird table is in keeping with its wild garden setting.

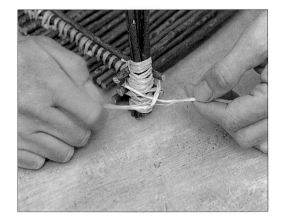

4 *Cut 32 lengths from the top of the osiers, each about 75cm/30in long. Divide these into four bundles of eight. Bind each bundle firmly at the bottom with raffia. Place the first bundle at one corner where the wall sticks project. Tie the bundle firmly to all the sticks. Repeat at the other three corners.*

5 *At the top, gather together the four bundles to create a wigwam shape and tie with raffia where they cross. Make a hanger by passing a few strands of raffia between the sticks, just under the raffia binding. Bring up and tie just above the binding, then tie the ends together for hanging.*

59

TRANSLUCENT LEAF LAMPSHADE

 Skeletonized leaves have a translucent, ethereal quality, and make delightful decorative materials. You can either skeletonize the leaves yourself or buy them – autumn is the time they become available. Here, they have been gilded so they stand out against a green-painted shade.

MATERIALS
decorator's sponge
green craft paint
plain fabric lampshade
picture framer's gilt wax
about 8 skeletonized leaves (or enough to go around the lampshade)
craft glue

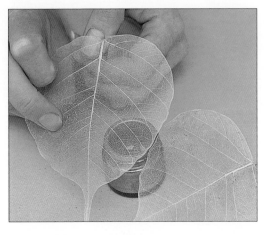

2 Using your fingers, rub picture framer's gilt wax on to the leaves. Try out the leaves in position on the lampshade until you are happy with the design.

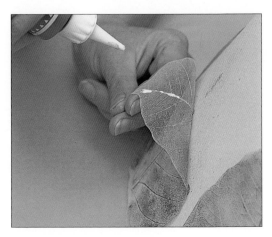

3 Apply glue sparingly to the back of a leaf and stick to the lampshade. Hold in position for a few seconds until the glue is dry.

1 Wet the sponge and squeeze out until just damp. Dip it into the paint, then wipe on to the lampshade.

4 Repeat with the other leaves until the lampshade is complete.

LEFT: Skeletonizing brings out the form of the leaves.

DRIED GRASS CIRCLET

 There's something beguiling about this simple circlet of dried grass — symbolic, perhaps, of food and life itself. In the long dark evenings of late autumn, there is more time to transform material dried during the summer into decorative pieces for the home.

MATERIALS
1m/39in gardener's wire
florist's (stem-wrap) tape
about 30 large grass heads, or more smaller ones
secateurs (pruners) or scissors
raffia

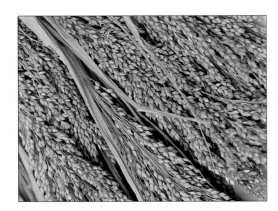

ABOVE: Choose the lushest grasses you can find, and don't cut off all the leaves as these lend texture to the finished piece.

1 Make a hook at each end of the wire, bend the wire into a circle and hook the ends together. Bind the circle with florist's (stem-wrap) tape.

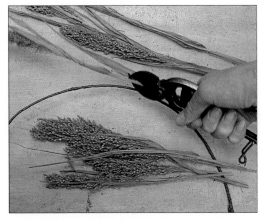

2 With a pair of sharp secateurs (pruners) cut the grass stems down to just below the first leaf from the top.

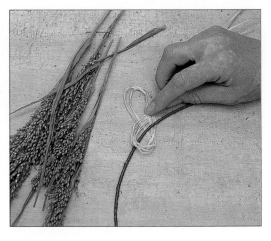

3 Fold a piece of raffia in half, pass both loose ends around the wire and back through the loop to fix (attach) it to the circlet.

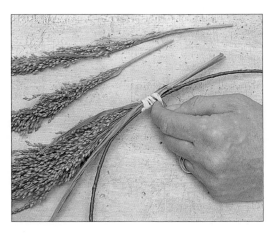

4 Take two grass heads and attach firmly with the raffia to the outside of the circlet, binding them at the top of the stems just under the seeds.

5 *About 7.5cm/3in along from the first binding, add two more heads to the inside of the circlet and bind. Repeat until the circlet is completely covered. Tie the ends of the raffia firmly to secure them.*

NOTE
Although grasses are very attractive, bear in mind that their green colour has a very short life, and most dry out to a warm, golden yellow colour. Always buy your grasses from a reputable dried flower supplier.

LEAF PRINT BOXES

Autumn leaves make delightful templates that can be used in a very simple way to decorate all manner of things. Choose interesting shapes, such as these deeply lobed oak leaves, and the end result is bound to be beautiful.

MATERIALS
plain cardboard box
matt emulsion (flat latex) paint in blue-grey
and cream
paintbrushes
pin oak leaf (*Quercus palustris*)
common oak leaf (*Quercus robur*)
stencil brush
newspaper
acrylic varnish

BELOW: This blue-grey and cream leaf colour combination makes an elegant alternative to more conventional autumn shades.

1 Paint the box inside and out with grey matt emulsion (flat latex) paint and allow to dry. Use the leaves to try out a design, and work out where you will place each motif.

2 Dip the tip of the stencil brush into the cream paint, then dab off the excess on a piece of scrap newspaper. Hold a large leaf on the side of the closed box and stipple the paint around its margins to make a clear imprint. Repeat all around the side of the box.

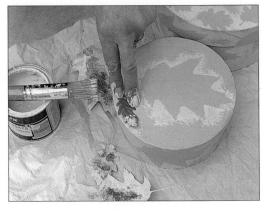

3 Repeat the large leaf motif in the middle of the top of the lid. Now use the small oak leaf in the same way to stencil a border around the top of the lid. Dab a little extra cream paint wherever there are large areas of grey between the leaves. Aim to apply a very thin veil of paint that allows the grey to show through, giving the impression of texture.

4 Once the paint is dry, apply a thin coat of varnish to all surfaces, inside and out, and allow to dry.

FALLING LEAF CURTAIN

A delightful sheer curtain with pockets for autumn leaves: the simple shapes of beech leaves have been used to complement the more elaborate oak leaves. It is very easy to make.

MATERIALS

scissors

white cotton organdie to fit window, plus three-quarters as much again for pockets and tabs

sewing machine

matching sewing thread

selection of autumn leaves

dressmaker's pins

curtain clips

1 Cut the organdie to fit the window, plus an allowance of 2.5cm/1in all around for the hem. Stitch a double hem all around. Lay the curtain on a flat surface and arrange the leaves on the curtain. Cut rectangles from the remaining organdie, a little larger than each leaf. Stitch a double hem around each piece.

NOTE

The autumn leaves in this project are naturally dried and therefore fully preserved. Although they are brittle, tucked into a sheer curtain that is not moved about, they are unlikely to get damaged.

LEFT: *Deeply lobed oak leaves make a pretty silhouette.*

2 Pin each rectangle over its leaf and stitch the two sides and the base, leaving the top free. The leaves will probably fall out during this process.

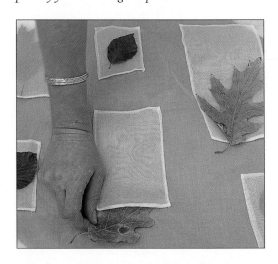

3 Replace each leaf in its pocket. Hang the curtain using curtain clips, or make tabs for the top edge.

ABOVE: The pockets are cut to fit each individual leaf and then the leaves are simply dropped into position.

SILVERY MIRROR FRAME

The glistening silvery medallions of honesty (*Lunaria*) (silver dollars) look wonderful woven into a dense frame for a mirror. The end result is light and delicate-looking while retaining an organic feel. Honesty grows prolifically in the hedgerows and, if allowed, in cottage-style gardens in temperate climates. The purple flowers of summer are replaced by uninspiring grey-looking medallion seedpods. However, when you remove the seedcases, you are left with a silvery membrane that makes a lovely decoration. It is far more resilient than it looks, but it is nevertheless best to use honesty where it won't have to stand up to daily wear and tear.

MATERIALS
garden wire
wire cutters
round mirror, ready-drilled, plus attachments
pliers
florist's (stem-wrap) tape
as much honesty (silver dollars) as you can collect
50cm/20in ivory organza

1 Cut enough wire to make a circle about 5cm/2in diameter smaller than the mirror. Make a hook at each end of the wire, join into a circle, then bind all of it.

2 Remove the seedcases from the honesty (silver dollars) and cut it into branched lengths of about 18cm/7in. Use the florist's (stem-wrap) tape to bind one length to the wire circle.

3 Place the next length of honesty a little lower than the first but so that the main stem lies over the main stem of the first piece. This way, you'll be able to create a dense mass of honesty. Continue to add lengths of honesty until the circle is completely covered. Next, you need to cover and bind the green-wrapped wire base.

4 Cut a strip of organza about 5cm/2in wide and thread it between the honesty medallions. Cut three lengths of garden wire 15cm/6in long. Bend the sharp cut ends in, then bind with a strip of organza.

5 Make a small forward-bending hook at one end, and hook this to the wire base of the wreath. Bend the wire over the top of the mirror. Repeat with the other two pieces of wire, positioning them near the bottom. Hang the mirror, and make a generous bow from the remaining organza to trim the wreath.

LEAF DECOUPAGE BIN

It is satisfying to use leaves in place of paper images for decoupage boxes, bins or even furniture. The trick is to press the leaves first to ensure they are very flat and, once they are stuck on, to use layer upon layer of varnish until the leaf looks as if it is part of the surface.

MATERIALS
acrylic craft paint in green and yellow
MDF (medium-density fibreboard) waste bin
paintbrushes
crackle glaze
PVA (white) glue
large pressed leaf
weights or books
acrylic varnish

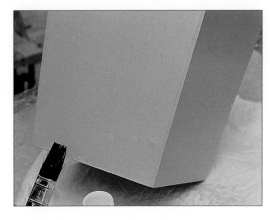

2 Different brands of crackle glaze are used in very different ways, so follow the manufacturer's instructions and try out the product first on the bottom of the bin. Paint one or two coats of crackle glaze on the outside of the bin. Allow to dry.

4 Apply PVA (white) glue to the back of the leaf, making sure you spread it to the very edges. Place the leaf in position, then rest heavy weights, such as books, on the leaf overnight. Remove the weights and allow the glue to dry fully.

1 Paint the bin inside and out with soft green paint and allow to dry.

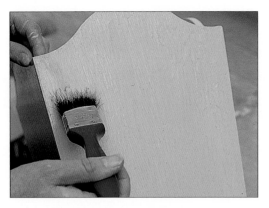

3 Very carefully lay on the second colour on the outside of the bin. The paint surface should crack as it dries. The size and type of cracks depend on the consistency of the top coat of paint.

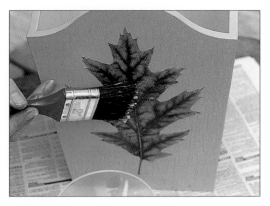

5 Coat all the surfaces with a thin coat of acrylic varnish. Allow to dry thoroughly. Repeat with as many coats of varnish as needed, until the leaf appears to be painted on to the bin.

FILIGREE CARVED PUMPKIN

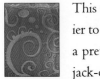 This delicate tracery pattern is easier to carve than it looks and makes a pretty alternative to traditional jack-o-lanterns. Make several and bring them to life by placing night-lights (tea-lights) inside to create a row of decorations.

MATERIALS
pen
pumpkin
pumpkin saw or craft knife saw
attachment
kitchen knife
scoop or spoon
lino (linoleum) cutting tools
night-light (tea-light)

1 Draw a wavy line around the top of the pumpkin to mark the edge of the lid then cut around this using the pumpkin saw. Use a sharp kitchen knife to cut out the centre of the lid for ventilation so that the lantern will burn while the lid is on.

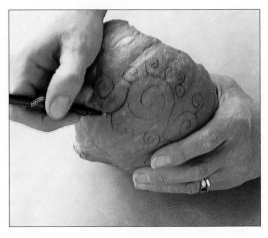

3 Draw an all-over tracery pattern on the skin of the pumpkin, working circles and curlicues freehand.

4 Use lino (linoleum) cutting tools in a range of thicknesses to cut out the pattern. Try out the night-light (tea-light) to check the light shines through. If not, scrape away a little more of the inside of the shell.

ABOVE: The wavy-edged lid is also given some simple decorative detailing.

2 Scoop out all the seeds and flesh using a kitchen spoon. Scrape away the inside to make a thin "shell".

SIMPLE PUMPKIN CARVING DESIGNS

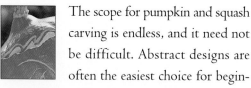 The scope for pumpkin and squash carving is endless, and it need not be difficult. Abstract designs are often the easiest choice for beginners as you really can't go wrong – all you need to do is simply add a few extra flourishes to fill in any gaps. Geometric designs are slightly more complicated as you need to plan them carefully to get full repeats around the whole circumference of the pumpkin.

The best solution is to divide the pumpkin into quarters or eighths from top to bottom, marking the divisions with a pen, and work out a design that can be repeated in each section.

Geometric designs can also be worked out along evenly marked-out concentric circles drawn out around the pumpkin.

Figurative designs look good on pumpkins, too. They don't have to be complicated – simple lines work well. If you're unsure about drawing freehand, photocopy a simple image, then reduce or enlarge it to fit the pumpkin. To transfer the image, pin the drawing or photocopy to the pumpkin, then mark out the design using a large needle or pricking tool to prick through the paper on to the skin of the pumpkin, following the lines of the image. Remove the paper, leaving a line of holes to carve along.

ABOVE: Witches are an alternative to jack-o-lanterns, while keeping to the traditional Halloween theme.

LEFT: Keep carving simple on smaller pumpkins, lending variety with slits, zig-zags and scrolls. Make several, then group them in a window display.

RIGHT: The peaceful features of this face make a simple but appealing image that is easy to transfer to a pumpkin. Lay her on a bed of leaves to give the impression of a woodland pillow.

ORGANIC CANDLE HOLDERS

 Autumn fruits and vegetables offer wonderful possibilities for organic candle holders. Many have firm flesh that provides good support for candles and night-lights (tea-lights). They must have a good stable base, to avoid the risk of falling over while the candle is burning and causing a fire. If the pieces you choose don't easily sit straight, use a kitchen knife to shave a little off the bottom so that it is flat. Even so, never leave any candles burning unattended, especially next to flammable surfaces.

BELOW: Apples make charming little candle holders, and this is a good way to use up windfalls (extras). First slice a little off the bottom of each one to create a stable base, then hollow the fruit out using an apple corer. Enlarge the hole a little so that it is big enough to accommodate a night-light (tea-light).

ABOVE: The "fingers" of the Crown of Thomas gourd seem to be cradling this pillar candle. Some gourds have very hard flesh, so you'll need a sharp knife to hollow them out. Wrap the candle in an autumn leaf, tie with raffia and place in the holder. (It is safe to burn only large diameter candles wrapped in leaves as the wax burns from the middle, leaving the outer surface cool.)

RIGHT: Small green striped squashes look charming holding apple-green candle stubs and set on rustic earthenware plates. They're quick and easy to prepare — simply hollow out the centre with an apple corer, then insert the candle.

PRESSED LEAF PICTURE FRAMES

The sepia tones of autumn leaves can be used to make very simple organic photograph frames. To produce sepia photographs of your family, use black-and-white film (XR2) and ask the processors to put it through the ordinary colour process (C41).

MATERIALS
photograph
oval mount
clip frame
selection of pressed leaves
secateurs (pruners) or scissors
craft glue

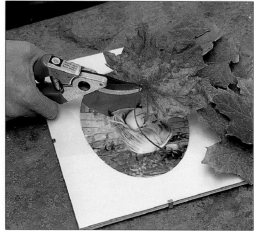

1 Position the photograph and mount in the frame. Collect together pressed leaves to cover the frame.

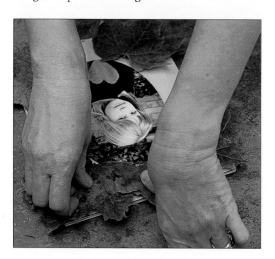

2 Snip the stems off the leaves and try out the arrangement around the frame.

LEFT: *Press leaves for at least a week before using.*

3 Run a line of craft glue down the spine of each leaf and glue in position on the glass over the mount.

4 The leaves may need to be held firmly until the glue is almost set. Continue gluing until the mount is completely covered with leaves.

WINTER'S FROSTY DAWN

Every leaf speaks bliss to me

Fluttering from the autumn tree

I shall smile when wreaths of snow

Blossom where the roses should grow;

EMILY BRONTË (1818-48)

ABOVE: A beautiful example of variegated holly leaves in all their glory.

LEFT: Hoar frost throws its translucent cloak of white over any remaining plant life, highlighting stems and veins.

Spreading his magnificent cloak of white over all that grows, Jack Frost announces winter is here. That beautiful first frosty morning sounds a silent death knell for autumn, putting deciduous plants to sleep for the winter. From now on, flowers will be few; fruits will be unable to survive and only the hardiest of berries will remain to provide colour for the garden.

This is the season when evergreens reign. Deep green and densely covered with needles, stately coniferous trees produce cones that range in size from little bigger than a plum stone (pit) to those that are fist-sized or even larger. Both branches and cones (pinecones) make brilliant craft materials, as do the glossy leaves of holly

BELOW: Frosted leaves reveal their delicate structure.

ABOVE: Stems of holly, stripped of their leaves, provide a fiery mass of colour in winter, especially if abundant branches are massed in a large jug.

and ivy. With this naturally lush and colourful fresh material, there is less need for dried or preserved material for decoration, but it does come into its own for making gifts.

Dried lavender, roses and spices can all be made into special scented treats for loved ones; the more brightly coloured dried flowers, such as yarrow, can be turned into a decoration that will recall an earlier, sunnier season.

The natural colours for decoration at this time of year are green and red. These can be lightened with variegated varieties of holly and ivy, which always add sparkle to arrangements. Variations on the red theme include fruits such as apples, cranberries and cut pomegranates which can be added to the berries of holly and pyracanthus that are readily available outside throughout the winter months.

RIGHT: Frosted grasses appear like sketchlines against the darker tones of the tree trunks.

BELOW: Frost dusts the contours of wild mushrooms, accentuating their shapes.

YARROW TREE

Yarrow (*Achillea millefolium*) dries beautifully, retaining its mellow old-gold tones. Each flower head provides a generous cushion of colour, making it very quick and easy to work with. Here, the dried seedheads of *Nigella orientalis* have been used to punctuate the yarrow for a rich textured look.

MATERIALS
kitchen knife
florist's dry foam block
yellow container
secateurs (pruners)
bundle of willow osiers (branches) or similar about 45cm/18in long
florist's dry foam ball 18cm/7in in diameter
raffia
3 large bunches dried yarrow
1 bunch *Nigella orientalis*
dried autumn leaves

VARIATION
Other dried flowers which are suitable to arrange in this way are: *Paeonia*, *Protea compacta*, *Rosa*, *Achillea ptarmica*, *Anaphalis margaritacea* and *Helichrysum*.

1 Trim the foam block to fit into the container. Use secateurs (pruners) to trim the sticks to an even length.

2 Hold the osiers (branches) in a bundle and drive them through the centre of the foam in the container. Push the florist's foam ball on to the osiers.

3 Bind the osiers with two strands of raffia and tie securely at the base.

4 Cut the yarrow stems to about 2.5cm/1in and push them into the foam so that it is completely covered and no foam is visible.

5 *Cut the* Nigella orientalis *stems to about 5cm/2in and add to the ball at intervals.*

6 *Arrange a selection of dried autumn leaves in the foam in the container to completely cover it providing texture and interest.*

NATURAL GIFTWRAP

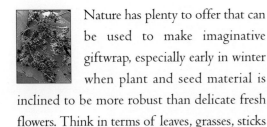

Nature has plenty to offer that can be used to make imaginative giftwrap, especially early in winter when plant and seed material is inclined to be more robust than delicate fresh flowers. Think in terms of leaves, grasses, sticks and twigs to create thoughtful but inexpensive decorations for wrappings. All these materials look best against the simplest of papers, such as ordinary brown parcel wrap or the soft tones and robust texture of recycled papers. You'll also need some basic cotton string, seagrass or other simple twine that tones well with natural materials to use as ties.

ABOVE: Dogwood twigs, with their fabulous burgundy colouring and uncomplicated straight lines, make a modern decoration for a brown paper package. The bundle has been tied together using a natural leather thong, then bound on to the parcel with the same thong for an understated, clean look.

LEFT: Each naturally giftwrapped parcel is unique yet they also look good together, as demonstrated by this highly individual trio.

ABOVE: A parcel simply wrapped in robust recycled paper and tied with seagrass string is given an individual finish with the addition of two stems of dried grass.

RIGHT: Larch twigs covered with lichen have a beauty all of their own, with the diminutive cones set against the glorious silvery grey of the lichen. If you don't own such a tree, a florist should be able to supply suitable twigs at this time of year. This parcel has been wrapped in recycled paper with a layer of translucent glycerine paper on top to provide an interesting layered background for the larch. The whole ensemble has been tied together with ordinary cotton string.

NATURAL CARDS

 Handmade greetings cards convey more heartfelt sentiments than the bought variety, and nature offers some of the most beautiful forms for inspiration. Early winter is an excellent time to find plant material for these, as much of it is already dried. Collect leaves, seedheads and seed-cases, dried flowers and twigs, and set out simple designs on recycled rag or bark papers.

LEFT: Use natural materials to create handmade greetings cards and gift tags.

ABOVE: Simple yet delightful, this card is emblazoned with a beech leaf cut into a heart shape and mounted on a background of honesty (silver dollars).

LEFT: Tiny dried chrysanthemums are set in a simple geometric arrangement on a square of natural fibre paper, positioned high on the rag paper "card" to relieve the squareness of the design. All the paper has been torn by hand, rather than cut, to give softer edges.

RIGHT: A sprig of oak, tied with gold paper twine and attached to bark paper, makes a charming gift tag.

BLUE SPRUCE AND AMARYLLIS GARLAND

 Deep pinks and raspberry shades are readily available in winter, and yet are often overlooked in a traditional preference for red. Here, the combination of frosty-looking blue spruce and lichen-covered twigs with translucent apple-green candles and the raspberry shades of the amaryllis and grapes, makes a refreshing winter colour scheme for a lavish garland.

MATERIALS
3 florist's foam blocks
kitchen knife
25cm/10in wide strip of chicken wire to fit mantel shelf
5 small metal buckets
secateurs (pruners)
2 branches blue spruce
glass nuggets or small pebbles
3 large green pillar candles
4 thin green pillar candles
fine raffia or twine
6 stems amaryllis (*Hippeastrum*)
10 sprays lichen-covered larch twigs
2 large bunches red grapes

RIGHT: Metal buckets hold candles and flowers, while adding to the silvery, frosty look.

1 Soak the florist's foam, cut each block in half lengthways and leave to drain. Arrange the cut blocks along the chicken wire. Wrap the chicken wire around the blocks leaving gaps for the buckets. Cut the spruce into manageable lengths and arrange in the florist's foam to create a base for the garland.

2 Place a large handful of glass nuggets or small pebbles in the bottom of each bucket, then secure one large candle in each of three of the buckets. Tie the thin candles into pairs using raffia or twine and set a pair in each of the remaining buckets. Add water, then two stems of amaryllis with each large candle.

3 Arrange the larch twigs amongst the spruce. Finally, split up the bunches of grapes and group some in front of each bucket.

ROSE AND SPICE POT-POURRI

The rich aromatic combination of sweet-smelling rose, lavender and spices, makes a warm and inviting winter pot-pourri. By fixing the aroma with orrisroot, you should be able to enjoy the perfume of the pot-pourri all winter long. If you want to give the scent an instant boost (as people are arriving for a party, for example), sprinkle on a few drops of hot water from the kettle.

MATERIALS

picture framer's gilt wax

7 cinnamon sticks cut into thirds

18 star anise

6ml/120 drops lavender essential oil

3ml/60 drops geranium essential oil

2ml/40 drops clove bud essential oil

small bottle

2.5ml/½tsp ground nutmeg

25g/1oz ground orrisroot

mixing containers

25g/1oz whole cloves

15g/½oz dried mace

115g/4oz dried lavender

225g/8oz dried rosebuds

1 Rub picture framer's gilt wax on to the cinnamon sticks and star anise, and reserve.

BELOW: *Choose pretty two-toned peach and yellow roses to add brightness to the finished pot-pourri.*

2 Blend the essential oils in a bottle and shake. Add a little oil to the ground nutmeg and orrisroot and blend. Add the rest of the blended oils to the whole dried spices. Cover and leave in a dark place for 24 hours.

3 In a large bowl, mix the cinnamon sticks and star anise with the remaining ingredients and add the essential oil mixture. Cover and leave for six weeks in a dark place before using or packing as a gift.

POMANDERS

Traditional pomanders can be given a new, less manicured look by substituting raffia for ribbon and trimming them with a variegated holly leaf. For centuries, pomanders have been cured with orrisroot and dried out over several weeks in a warm dry place, such as an airing cupboard. The quicker alternative method is to dry them in the oven; although the pomanders are preserved this way, they come out a little softer than by the traditional method.

MATERIALS

soft-skinned oranges, such as navel

sharp vegetable knife

cloves

skewer

raffia

variegated holly leaves

1 Preheat the oven to 110°C/225°F/Gas ¼. Make slits in the skins of the oranges using a small sharp vegetable knife. This helps speed the drying process in the oven. Put a line of cloves either side of the slit. Continue to build up the design by making a row of cloves around the middle of the pomander, with another row either side of that.

> ### TIP
> If you are planning a geometric design, make slits at each quarter. If you wish to work a motif you may prefer to leave the front of the orange intact, and just make a slit in each side and one at the back. Geometric designs look good when the slits become part of the pattern.

LEFT: Ring the changes from the normal geometric shapes and make heart and star shapes instead.

2 Fill in the top and bottom of the orange with concentric circles of cloves.

3 Pass a skewer through the slits of the oranges and balance the skewer ends on the sides of a deep dish so that plenty of air can circulate around the oranges. Place the dish in the oven and leave for 12 hours, or until the oranges are completely dry. Tie a length of raffia around the pomander, making a hanging loop, and tuck a sprig of holly into the top.

APPLE AND IVY TABLE DISPLAY

Shiny ruby-toned apples teamed with glossy berried ivy offer a bold alternative way to create the traditional winter colour scheme of green and red. Crab apples have been used to add extra detail to the arrangement.

MATERIALS
urn

plastic sheet

florist's foam block

kitchen knife

heavy-gauge stub (floral) wires

about 16 red apples

2 branches of crab apples

secateurs (pruners)

berried ivy sprigs

BELOW: Soft raspberry-coloured candles perfectly complement the colours of the apples.

1 Line the urn with a plastic sheet, soak the florist's foam, drain, then cut to fit tightly into the urn. Pass a stub (floral) wire through each apple and twist the ends together.

2 Make a circle of apples around the rim of the urn, securing them in the florist's foam with the wires. Make a second ring of apples on top of the first, then add one on top to create a dome.

3 Wire up the clusters of crab apples and add to the arrangement, positioning them in between the larger red apples. Trim the berried ivy stems and insert the stems into the foam.

4 Fill in any remaining gaps in the display with more wired crab apples.

HOLLY AND POMEGRANATE SIDE DISPLAY

Pomegranates are wonderfully visual winter fruits, especially when cut open to show off their glistening clusters of ruby seeds. Here, a classic winter display is given a new twist by choosing variegated holly and nature's own baubles in the form of pomegranates.

MATERIALS
florist's foam blocks
large shallow bowl
large bunch of variegated holly
secateurs (pruners)
bunch of holly berries (*Ilex verticillata*)
knife
6 pomegranates
24 heavy-gauge stub (floral) wires

ABOVE: Quartered pomegranates add a jewel-like quality to seasonal holly.

1 Soak the florist's foam, drain it and place in the bowl. Position a long piece of holly at the back of the arrangement and one at each side to create a fan shape.

2 Fill in with plenty of holly, trimming the stems to create a domed shape. Add stems of holly berries throughout the arrangement.

3 Quarter the pomegranates lengthways and pierce each one with a stub (floral) wire through the bottom end. Bend the end of the wire to secure.

4 Position the pomegranates carefully, inserting the wires into the florist's foam and bending them into position if necessary.

CRANBERRY HEART

 This glossy red heart made from cranberries and raffia has a wonderful contemporary feel. Cranberries are easy to find from late autumn right into the middle of winter. They retain their shiny brightness well for several weeks, though as the berries dry they will shrink a little.

MATERIALS
wire cutters
1m/39in garden wire
1 large punnet of cranberries
florist's reel wire
raffia

2 Bend the two circles into heart shapes. Put one heart shape inside the other and bind them together top and bottom using florist's reel wire.

3 Bind the hearts together using raffia, passing the raffia between the cranberries. Use the raffia to make a hanging loop at the top.

1 Cut the garden wire in half and make a small hook at one end. Thread cranberries on to the other end. When the wire is filled, make another hook and join together. Repeat with the other piece of wire.

WINTER'S SWEET REPOSE

And Winter slumbering in the open air,
Wears on his smiling face a dream of Spring!
SAMUEL TAYLOR COLERIDGE (1772-1834)

ABOVE: Winter jasmine produces surprisingly delicate-looking, but nevertheless hardy, yellow flowers on leafless stems all through the winter and into spring.

LEFT: A metal garden basket full of variegated holly brings seasonal cheer to the coldest of days.

As winter presses on and the landscape retreats under a blanket of snow, dark evenings are the time to use dried material from the more abundant months. Dried beans, preserved leaves and flowers can all be made into gifts and decorations. The evergreens are still around, of course, and the traditional hollies and ivies can be supplemented with softer-toned eucalyptus for a lighter effect.

As the weeks progress, just as we're lulled into the impression that nature really has entered an everlasting sleep, she surprises us with flowers: winter-flowering jasmine (*Jasminum nudiflorum*) sprouts tiny golden blooms on green shoots whenever there's a mild spell in winter, right through to spring. Long-lasting hellebores, with their delicate nodding heads and subtle shades that span white to green, palest pink to softest burgundy, make their appearance late in winter

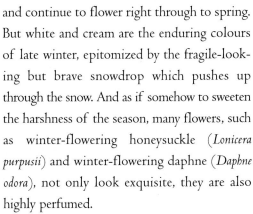

ABOVE: The waxy, white flowers of Helleborus niger *are winter's natural stars.*

and continue to flower right through to spring. But white and cream are the enduring colours of late winter, epitomized by the fragile-looking but brave snowdrop which pushes up through the snow. And as if somehow to sweeten the harshness of the season, many flowers, such as winter-flowering honeysuckle (*Lonicera purpusii*) and winter-flowering daphne (*Daphne odora*), not only look exquisite, they are also highly perfumed.

LEFT: Even in the depths of winter, nature provides colour and structure to the countryside.

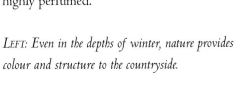

ABOVE: Snow carpets the countryside, providing warmth and protection from harsh frosts.

In the deepest of winter, follow nature's lead and decorate your home using the purest of white flowers that will scent as well as decorate the room. Enhance their purity by displaying them in white containers that will also reflect the pale wintry light.

Plant up some of the early flowering bulbs to enjoy inside – as their vigorous shoots push through the earth, they are a symbolic reminder of the work nature is putting in behind the scenes. Soon this energy will be echoed outside as the first spring shoots appear. In the meantime, relish the burgeoning of life indoors and, when the bulbs do open, enjoy their heady natural scent.

EUCALYPTUS AND WHITE HELLEBORE RING

 The blue-green leaves of eucalyptus have a frosty appeal, especially when teamed with seasonal white flowers such as these exquisitely beautiful hellebores (*Helleborus niger*). If you're unable to find these, you could substitute white anemones for a similar effect.

MATERIALS
kitchen knife
florist's foam ball, 18cm/7in minimum
diameter
23cm/9in plate
4 church candles, 2.5cm/1in in diameter
scissors
bunch of small-leaved eucalyptus
16 *Helleborus niger* or white anemones

1 Cut the foam ball in half — or slice off a section if it is larger — to fit the plate. Soak it in water and allow to drain. Using the kitchen knife, cut the bottom ends off three of the candles to create varying lengths and snip the wicks with scissors. Push the candles into the centre of the foam.

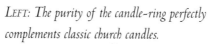

LEFT: *The purity of the candle-ring perfectly complements classic church candles.*

2 Cut the eucalyptus into pieces about 15cm/6in long and arrange in the foam to cover it.

3 Cut the hellebore flower stems to about 12.5cm/5in long and add to the arrangement at random intervals.

EUCALYPTUS STAR

The pretty evergreen leaves of eucalyptus dry well, retaining their colour, though reducing slightly in size. This delicate star makes an attractive winter decoration that will gradually dry out and last for weeks.

MATERIALS

12 willow osiers (branches) about
60cm/24in long
secateurs (pruners)
florist's reel wire
small-leafed eucalyptus

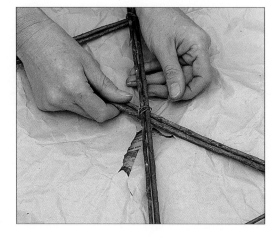

2 Place one triangle over the other to make a star shape and wire them together at all the points where the triangles cross.

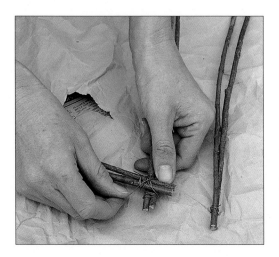

1 Trim the osiers (branches) to the same length and wire in pairs at each end. Wire three pairs of osiers together, making a triangle. Repeat with the other pairs.

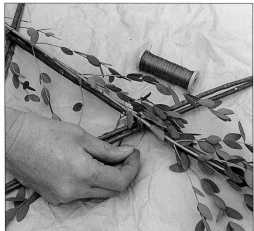

3 Wire lengths of eucalyptus to the willow to cover the star, but create a feathery finished effect.

WINTER CHANDELIER

Variegated holly always looks pretty and makes a robust yet delightful decoration for this wild winter chandelier. Here, thornless holly from the tops of the trees has been used as it is much easier to work with.

MATERIALS
large cones to fill the basket
newspaper
antique gold spray paint
ornate wire basket
variegated holly branches
secateurs (pruners)
florist's reel wire

2 Choose young branches of holly with small offshoots and fix them to the basket rim using florist's reel wire. The offshoots give depth to the rim.

1 First gild the cones. This should be done in a well-ventilated area. Shake the can well, then spray the cones and allow to dry. Place in the basket.

3 Using florist's reel wire, attach a generous sprig to the bottom of the basket.

EUCALYPTUS PYRAMID

 This pretty pyramid of eucalyptus, set on a footed glass dish, makes a simple but impressive table display that's quick and easy to make. This pyramid has a dry foam base: the eucalyptus will go on looking fresh for a day or two, then gradually dry out for an everlasting arrangement.

MATERIALS
florist's foam cone, 20cm/8in high
footed glass dish
secateurs (pruners)
small-leaved eucalyptus sprigs
eucalyptus buds

2 Work up the cone, positioning the eucalyptus sprigs at a more upright angle as you work nearer to the top.

1 Place the foam cone on the footed dish, then cut some sprays of eucalyptus and arrange around the base.

3 When the cone is completely covered with foliage, add the frosty looking eucalyptus buds.

DRIED BEAN MOSAIC

Dried beans come in a glorious variety of shapes, sizes and colours, and make ideal material for a natural mosaic. The key to success is to work in concentric circles or straight lines.

MATERIALS
scissors

paper

14cm/5in square picture frame

pen

craft glue

mung beans

haricot beans (navy beans)

1 Cut a square of paper the same size as the frame back. Fold it in half and draw and cut out half a heart shape. At its widest points, the heart should be about 1.5cm/⅝in smaller than the frame. Position the heart centrally on the backing paper and draw around it.

2 Squeeze a line of craft glue along the drawn line.

LEFT: Two different sizes of bean contrast strikingly in this simple mosaic.

3 Very carefully stick a line of mung beans along the line of glue. Squeeze another line of glue inside this and make another line of mung beans. Continue in this way, working in concentric rounds, until the whole heart is covered.

4 Squeeze a line of glue around the outside of the heart and make a line of haricot beans (navy beans). Make another line outside this, then fill in the corners, laying on one bean at a time. Mount in the picture frame.

DRIED ROSE LOVE TOKEN

Heart shapes are always appealing and this one, made from preserved green beech leaves and dried gold-coloured rosebuds, makes a delightful gift and a lasting decoration for anywhere in the house.

MATERIALS

75cm/30in garden wire

pliers

florist's (stem-wrap) tape

florist's reel wire

sprigs of preserved beech leaves

12 dried yellow rosebuds

2 Bend the circle into a heart shape.

4 Cut 12 lengths of reel wire 5cm/2in long, and pass each one through the base of a dried rosebud. Twist the ends together.

1 Bend the length of garden wire into a circle, hooking the ends together. Bind the wire circle with the florist's (stem-wrap) tape.

3 Use florist's reel wire to attach the beech sprigs to the heart shape, bending the twigs to follow the shape as you wire them.

5 Wire the yellow rosebuds to the base, tucking in the wire ends at the back of the heart to create a neat finished piece.

EVERLASTING LEAF AND FLOWER ORBS

Leafy balls make delightful organic decorations. These have been made from preserved beech and oak leaves and preserved hydrangea flowers. Beech leaves are used as the base for the flower ball. For the leaf balls, simply rub the leaves first with a little picture framer's gilt wax, then follow the first two steps.

MATERIALS

picture framer's gilt wax
preserved beech leaves
glue gun and glue sticks
florist's dry foam ball 10cm/4in in diameter
preserved hydrangea heads
scissors

1 Apply a line of glue down the centre of a beech leaf and stick it to the foam ball. Repeat, to make a line of leaves around the circumference of the ball.

2 Filling in one side at a time, cover the ball completely with beech leaves.

LEFT: Enhance the autumnal shades with toning ribbon.

3 Rub the hydrangea florets with a little picture framer's gilt wax. Carefully snip the florets off their stems, leaving about 3mm (⅛in) stem.

4 Place a small blob of glue in the centre back of each flower and attach on top of the leaves, allowing the petals to curl naturally at the edges to give texture to the finished piece.

WINTER WINDOW DECORATIONS

In winter, when light is precious, make a feature of your windows. Either bring in a little nature (in the form of branches or evergreen leaves) from outside and team it with candlelit lanterns to extend the light into the dusk, or seek out the whitest flowers you can find to bring lightness to the windowsills. Remember too that many white flowers in winter have beautiful scent. As winter progresses, there will be several varieties to choose from, such as snowdrops, paper-white narcissi and *Helleborus niger*.

BELOW: Bring brightness to a lichen-covered larch twig by rubbing picture framer's silver wax on to the cones. Hang the twigs at the window using string. Complete the display with a row of lanterns. For safety's sake, never leave lighted lanterns unattended, and don't draw curtains in front of them.

ABOVE: Trim window handles with a bouquet of paper-white narcissi: small bunches are tucked into orchid phials (vials) that have been wrapped in translucent organza ribbon.

RIGHT: Make a display of white flowers and vases for brightness on the windowsill.

WINTER POSIES

Although in the dead of winter few plants are in bloom, there are some that produce modest flowers, and these are all the more beautiful for their rarity. White is the favourite colour for late winter – notably, classic snowdrops and hellebores (*Helleborus niger*). Posies of the palest blooms, or grey-green foliage that looks as if it has been touched by frost, evoke the silent peacefulness of a crisp, clear winter's day when the landscape has been blanketed with snow. Their almost colourless petals seem to complement the gentle watery light of midwinter and inspire hope of the spring to come.

BELOW: Eucalyptus produces frosty-looking buds. Wrap them up with sprays of foliage in translucent glycerine paper to make a pretty winter bouquet.

ABOVE: White anemones fade to a fabulous antique ecru shade. Tie them with a toning ribbon and arrange them in a cream-coloured cup and saucer.

RIGHT: Exquisitely beautiful white hellebores (Helleborus niger) are all the more treasured as they are one of the few flowers to bloom in the dead of winter. However, they stay around long enough (well into spring) to be really appreciated and last well as cut flowers too. Make a feature of them by incorporating them in a display of glass and candles.

WINTER BULB DISPLAYS

Perhaps because there is so little evidence of life amongst plants in winter, the first shoots are all the more precious. As winter draws on, bulbs planted for indoor displays begin to shoot. For bulbs to flower earlier than in the ground you must plant them in the autumn and keep in a warm, dark place for about six weeks to encourage them to sprout. If you forgot to plant them up in autumn, look around florists and markets for pots planted with paper-white narcissi or hyacinths, then re-plant them in your own displays. They look wonderful even while they are still green, the vigorous shoots holding the promise of exquisite perfumed blooms. Once they are planted, it is astounding quite how fast they grow and the tall slender leaves look wonderful, even before the blooms appear.

ABOVE: Secure the leaves in position using florist's wire bent into a hairpin shape.

LEFT: A covering of autumn leaves over the top of narcissi bulbs will both protect the bulbs against the cold and make a decorative topping while the shoots are still opening out.

ABOVE: Hyacinths look wonderful planted one to a pot, then arranged in pairs or larger groups.

RIGHT: Hyacinths are quite happy without compost as long as their roots are kept in water. Set them in glass jars for a light effect that shows off their delicate translucent roots. A ring of autumn leaves tucked around the bulb makes a pretty "collar".

125

SUPPLIERS

UK

THE HOP SHOP
Castle Farm
Shoreham
Sevenoaks
Kent TN14 7UR
Tel: 01959 523219

NORFOLK LAVENDER
Caley Mill
Heacham
King's Lynn
Norfolk PE31 7JE
Tel: 01485 570384
Dried lavender, lavender
essential oil.

NEAL'S YARD REMEDIES
12 Chelsea Farmer's' Market
Sydney Street
London SW3
Tel: 0171 498 1686 for other
stores and stockists.
Essential oils, dried lavender,
dried roses, rosebuds, orrisroot.

TUDOR ROSE
Thomas Nurseries
273 Sutton Common Road
Sutton
Surrey
Tel: 0181 288 0999
Dried flowers and florist's
equipment.

USA

DODY LYNESS CO.
7336 Berry Hill Dr.
Palos Verdes Peninsula
CA 90274
Tel: (310) 377-7040
Suppliers of pot-pourri,
fragrance oils, dried blossoms,
herbs, spices, dried and
pressed flowers.

HERB SHOPPE
215 W. Main St.
Greenwood IN 46142
Tel: (317) 889-3495
Suppliers of bulk herbs,
pot-pourri supplies, and
essential oils.

GAILANN'S FLORAL CATALOG
821 W. Atlantic St.
Branson MO 65616
Offers a full line of floral
supplies and dried flowers.

TOM THUMB WORKSHOPS
PO Box 357
Mappsville VA 32407
Tel: (804) 8245-3507
Suppliers of dried flowers,
containers, ribbons, floral items,
spices, herbs and essential oils.

AUSTRALIA

HEDGEROW FLOWERS
177 King William Road
Hyde Park
SA 5061
Tel: (08) 373-4499

ACKNOWLEDGEMENTS
Let the beauty of nature take the glory for
this book as its very essence depends on
the wonderful colours, shapes and forms in
the world around us. I have had the
privilege of working with these, the best
materials available and, I hope, perhaps
passed on a little of my enthusiasm for all
things natural. Thank you to Debbie,
whose exquisite photographs have captured
this natural beauty, and to her baby Fin,
whose delayed arrival meant we could work
right into the winter. Thank you, too, to
Helen, who has transformed the material
into a brilliant production, and been so
supportive of both Debbie and me.
The carved pumpkins were supplied by
Mary Maguire and Deborah Schneebeli-
Morrell.

INDEX

PUBLISHERS' NOTE:
The Publishers would like to thank
Wildlife and Garden Matters Picture
Library for permission to reproduce the
following pictures in this book: p80,
p83 right, p105.